A Year in the Life of Sheppey

2011

A Photographic Record of the Island's Everyday Life
365 images captured by local photographers

Kent Creative Arts CIC

A Year in the Life of Sheppey
2011

Kent Creative Arts CIC
www.kentcreativearts.co.uk

Copyright © Kent Creative Arts CIC 2012

Photographs Copyright © the Photographers 2012

Book Design: Bob Lamoon
www.boblamoon.com

Printed by Printworks Int. Ltd (Hong Kong / London)

ISBN 978-0-9569562-2-4

Our Platinum Sponsors

Our Gold Sponsors

Our Silver Sponsors

Our Bronze Sponsors

Victor Hire Ltd.

Introduction

As the title suggests, this book reflects on a year in the life of the Isle of Sheppey. It is published on the occasion of the exhibition held at Castle Connections in Queenborough from 21st to 23rd September 2012. This is the first volume published on the island.

The whole 365 project is the result of a collective work, where individuals submitted photographs during the year 2011, capturing glimpses of life around them. When it started, I was interested in what people would do to contribute. I found quite astonishing the amount of creative talent that has come out of it. As a commitment to the idea of community photography, it is designed not only to reveal, define and preserve the island's identity but also to help change the way people relate to the place they live in and appreciate it.

A Year in the Life of Sheppey brings together the work of 29 photographers through 365 photographs – one for each day of the year - selected by a judging panel out of 1476 pictures submitted by 44 photographers. It shows the different ways in which to capture Sheppey, the well known as well as the less reported aspects of life. The photographs offer an opportunity to see the work of amateurs alongside the work of established photographers.

365 combines the objectivity of documentary with a reflective and artistic approach. The result is fragmented information about life, telling a story visually and revealing a proud community. The subjects covered by the photographers are extremely diverse. Their photographs explore what people do at home and at work, presenting day-to-day life as it is lived. They also describe the colourful way they entertain themselves. The pictures capture other moments too, objects and landscapes. This diversity demonstrates the various ways the photographers observe aspects of their community.

Along the way, the photographs remind us of how much we have to lose. The island around us is changing, with traditional characteristics slowly disappearing, buildings being built and destroyed, people coming and going. So these images become part of our visual heritage. They make us aware and create things to think about.

This book is designed to take you on a journey through Sheppey and I hope it will be a pleasant one.

I would like to thank the photographers whose commitment over the year has been fantastic. This is their work. I am also immensely grateful to all those individuals who have helped, to our sponsors and funders. It wouldn't have been possible without them.

Nathalie Banaigs   Project Manager

James Apps

Driftwood

Richard Jeferies

Chris Reed

Telescope Alley, Sheerness, cat sitting on aviary

Richard Jeferies

St Helens Road, Sheerness   Wednesday 5th January

Richard Jeferies

Richard Jeferies

Running, alley near James Street, Sheerness

Friday 7th January

Richard Jeferies

Light Beams, the A249, Sheerness Bridge

Kerr Jeferies

Trevor Jones

Warden Bay towards Leysdown

Jo Eden

Jo Eden

Richard Jeferies

Linda Brinklow

Swan light, Bartons Point

Richard Jeferies

This page has been sponsored by Jo Eden. For my husband Ray's birthday.

David Gethin

Sheerness beach near Marine Parade

Chris Reed

Chris Reed

Chris Reed

Moonlight on Warden Bay Wednesday 19th January

Jo Eden

The sun setting behind the two bridges
on the Isle of Sheppey

Chris Reed

Chris Reed

Sheppey rugby team beating Beckenham

Chris Reed

Jo Eden

Chris Reed

Train waiting to leave at Sheerness train station

Tuesday 25th January

Chris Reed

'Spring is on it's way'
Sheerness by the Clock-tower

Jo Eden

Exercising to keep warm
Jonathan on the cross trainer

Sheppey Speaking Up Group

'Starting to fly' The new Primary School being built, Warden Bay Road

Jo Eden

James Apps

Bottling off The Leas

Trevor Jones

Jo Eden

The Lovely Lady of Bruell Way

James Apps

Jo Eden

'Raspberry Ripple' Leysdown

Jo Eden

Bob Collins, Sheppey Artist delivering a painting to the Dockyard exhibition

Friday 4th February

James Apps

'A man happy in his job'
Paul Hayes of Halfway Post Office

James Apps

Trevor Jones

View over Sheerness to the Steel Works

James Apps

Charlotte Huggins

James Apps

Pear Tree Cottage in the rain

Thursday 10th February

James Apps

The old Dockyard Defences

James Apps

Jo Eden

Amusements at Leysdown

James Apps

Trevor Jones

Work in progress, Sheppey Little Theatre

Linda Rogout

From Abbey Rise Field, Minster
looking towards Southend

Wednesday 16th February

Linda Rogout

Thursday 17th February

'Drake's Wake'
The Slacks, Warden beach

Jo Eden

Trine in her shop, Daisy Chains, Sheerness Friday 18th February

Jo Eden

Charlotte Huggins

Geese rising from the sea, Shellness Beach

James Apps

Street furniture

Marlies Haselton

Sand pit, Sheerness   Tuesday 22nd February

Charlotte Huggins

Charlotte Huggins

'Sunset Drive'
Imperial Drive towards Donkey Hill, Warden

Thursday 24th February

Jo Eden

The new school progresses
Warden Bay Road, Warden

Jo Eden

Up on the roof, almost
Sheppey Little Theatre

Linda Rogout

Shellness Hamlet

James Apps

Jo Eden

Kent Fire and Rescue launch under the Kingsferry Bridge

Jo Eden

Marlie Haselton

'Waiting for his ticket'
Marine Parade, Sheerness

Marlies Haselton

Jo Eden

'Welcome to Sheppey'

Caroline Price

Linda Brinklow

Kyle on his stunt bike

Caroline Price

Steel Mill in town

Caroline Price

'Lift off' Leysdown beach   Thursday 10th March

Jo Eden

The Abbey Gatehouse
From the entrance to the Abbey Hall

Linda Rogout

Richard Jeferies

Jo Eden

Richard Jeferies

'Burnt Leaves'
The woods, Warden Springs Caravan Park

Jo Eden

Catholic Church, Broadway, Sheerness   Wednesday 16th March

Richard Jeferies

'My pear tree has awoken'

Caroline Price

Jo Eden

'Rebuilt' Sheerness windmill

Jo Eden

Holy Well of St Sexburgha
Peter and Maria's garden, Minster

Sunday 20th March

Jo Eden

Jo Eden

'Who pays the Ferryman?'
Where the Harty ferry used to cross to Oare

Jo Eden

Jo Eden

'Drawing water' Leysdown Bay   Thursday 24th March

Jo Eden

Friday 25th March

'Misty bridge'
A reminder of the 'Three Billy Goats Gruff'

Marlies Heselton

Jo Eden

Sudi, Jasmine and Laure
Flynns Bee Farms, Brambledown

Jo Eden

Linda Rogout

'Cheerful bicycle' High Street, Sheerness

Marlies Heselton

'Sails' Warden Bay   Wednesday 30th March

Jo Eden

Jo Eden

Jo Eden

'Good Shepherd' St Thomas Church, Harty

Marlies Haselton

David Gethin

Spring in the Council Gardens

Linda Rogout

Linda Rogout

'Big Skies' Warden

Jo Eden

Trevor Jones

'In the treetops'
From Rowetts Way over Eastchurch

Jo Eden

'A study in red'
Ferry Road from the top deck of a bus

Linda Rogout

Piped outlet on the Swale
between the Bridge and Rushenden

James Apps

Jo Eden

'Under Wraps' Russell Street

Linda Rogout

James Apps

'Table for One, Sir?' Garden in Minster

Linda Rogout

James Apps

Fun fair ride, Leysdown

Jeremy Sage

Linda Rogout

Rex Piles

'In the Frame' Derek Friday
Chairman of the Sheppey Little Theatre

Tuesday 19th April

Linda Rogout

Wednesday 20th April   'A packed beach' Leysdown

Jo Eden

Linda Brinklow

Friday 22nd April   'Texture and light'

Caroline Price

My daughter reading to George the guinea pig
James Street, Sheerness

Richard Jeferies

This page has been sponsored by Sittingbourne and Sheppey Conservative Association
in celebration of St George's Day

'A crooked house' Warden Point

Richard Jeferies

James Apps

Mother and lamb, Minster

Linda Brinklow

Canal crossing, Sheerness

Wednesday 27th April

Richard Jeferies

Richard Jeferies

Linda Brinklow

Trevor Jones

'Tea party' The Spinney, Leysdown   Sunday 1st May

Jo Eden

Marlies Haselton

Caroline Price

Caroline Price

'Best graffiti ever'
Environment Agency sign, Outside the Lifeguard Hut

Thursday 5th May

Katy Jackson

Friday 6th May   'Thirsty duck' Sheerness Beach

Marlies Haselton

Jo Eden

Trevor Jones

New LED lights, Scrapsgate Road, Minster   Monday 9th May

Linda Rogout

'A Reminder'
Coast Road approaching The White House

Linda Rogout

Windmill from our bedroom window
Sheerness

Wednesday 11th May

Kerry and Ricky March

'In the pink'
Victoria's bungalow 'Water Gypsy' Warden

Jo Eden

Trevor Jones

'School's Out' Sheppey College Car Park

Linda Rogout

Trevor Jones

Kerry and Ricky March

Marlies Haselton

Minster beach from Baldwin Road

Kerry and Ricky March

Caroline Price

Linda Brinklow

Kings Ferry Bridge & the Sheppey Crossing from Elmley Marshes

Saturday 21st May

Carolin Galvin

Linda Brinklow

Crawford Centre

Tuesday 24th May

Whilst out with my friend along the canal by Edenbridge Drive

Gary, Crawford Centre

Paul Hoggins

'Enjoying a walk' Bartons Point
"This is something we like to do in our photo session"

Crawford Centre

'Shall We Dance?'
Jack and Poppy, Barton's Point, Sheerness

Paul Hoggins

Linda Rogout

James Apps

'Progress but at what price?'
Cowstead Corner, Sheppey Way

James Apps

James Apps

House Sparrow feeding family

James Apps

Linda Brinklow

James Apps

Linda Rogout

This page has been sponsored by Linda Rogout for her parents Hilda and Ted

Julia McDougall

Carolin Galvin

The entrance to Sheerness seafront

Julia McDougall

Trevor Jones

Amanda works out on the seafront at Sheerness

Paul Hoggins

Julia McDougall

Saturday 11th June

'Buttresses and Corbels'
The old water tower, Trinity Road, Sheerness

Linda Rogout

Paul Hoggins

Moon Rise over Halfway, Halfway Road

Linda Rogout

Linda Rogout

Breakneck Hill, The Broadway, Minster

Linda Rogout

Kerry and Ricky March

Daniel Nash

James Apps

James Apps

James Apps

Collared Dove nesting in an old TV aerial

James Apps

James Apps

Melvyn Ingram

Linda Rogout

Time to wallpaper in Sheerness

Julia McDougall

Julia McDougall

Monday 27th June

'Clover Field'
Abbey Rise field, looking towards Minster Road

Linda Rogout

Linda Rogout

'Mad Mike investigates banana tree pre labelled for market'

Julia McDougall

Linda Brinklow

'Pathway to ...?' Field of wheat at Halfway

Carolin Galvin

James Apps

James Apps

Clive Ballard

James Apps

James Apps

Trevor Jones

James Apps

Julia McDougall

Trevor Jones

'Geranium Explosion of Colour'
Sheerness Swimming Pool

Julia McDougall

Trevor Jones

Julia McDougall

Rides Mill, Sheerness
Restored after arson attack

Julia McDougall

Carolin Galvin

James Apps

Blessing of the waters, Queenborough

Linda Brinklow

Julia McDougall

'A view into a past time'
Naval Dockyard Church Blue Town

Julia McDougall

Mick Kenton
BRFM new studios at the Pavilion, Sheerness

Wednesday 20th July

Julia McDougall

'Ice cream, then a walk on the seawall'
Sheerness

Julia McDougall

The only visible sign of the Redan Café
once located next to Sheerness Jetty

Friday 22nd July

Julia McDougall

Melvyn Ingram

Visiting Bell Ringers ring out the chimes
All Saints, Eastchurch

Sunday 24th July

James Apps

Marlies Haselton

James Apps

'The Decisive Moment' Eli and Woody
Sheerness Seafront near the IOS Yacht Club

Paul Hoggins

James Apps

The Trafalgar, Queenborough, made pretty

James Apps

Linda Brinklow

Chris Reed

Nikki Coppins

Charlotte Huggins

Caroline Price

'Just good friends'
Gerry & Peter at a Big Fish Arts' Party

Chris Reed

Marlies Haselton

Ted, from Halfway. A volunteer
litter picker for fifty years

James Apps

Richard Jeferies

'Moody Blues' from Minster Leas

James Apps

James Apps

Kaj Steffensen

Fiona Jeferies

The owner and staff of Ali's cafe

Charlotte Huggins

Linda Rogout

The Church of St. Henry and St. Elizabeth
Sheerness

Linda Rogout

Linda Rogout

Linda Rogout

Feeding the swans and cygnets
Barton's Point, Sheerness

Paul Hoggins

Linda Rogout

Charlotte Huggins

'Another Hole in the Road'
Minster Road and Barton Hill Drive

Linda Rogout

Linda Rogout

'The flag must be flown' Leysdown

James Apps

James Apps

James Apps

James Apps

Friday 26th August   Warning sign at the Healthy Living Centre

James Apps

Julia McDougall

Julia McDougall

Marlies Haselton

Julia McDougall

Tracey using the free exercise facilities
The Leas, Minster

Julia McDougall

The old school house at Elmley
The village that died

Julia McDougall

Julia McDougall

'Off to Sea' The Promenade, Sheerness

Linda Rogout

'Once was Holy'
The Old Church, Naval Terrace, Blue Town

Sunday 4th September

James Apps

Monday 5th September   'Open Doors, Open Day'

James Apps

James Apps

Great Mill, Sheerness, from Wood Street

Carolin Galvin

A reflected view of the Kings Ferry Bridge and The Sheppey Crossing

Thursday 8th September

Carolin Galvin

Daniel Nash, BRFM, interviews Dan Cruickshank
Sheppey Little Theatre

Linda Rogout

From the roof of Shurland Hall Gatehouse   Saturday 10th September

Julia McDougall

'Sleepy Sunday'
Sheerness Town Centre just before 8am

Carolin Galvin

The gardens by the Leisure Centre, Sheerness   Monday 12th September

Linda Rogout

'Beacon Of Light'
Minster Beach beacon at sun rise

Carolin Galvin

Linda Rogout

Marlies Haselton

Rex Piles

'Where there's rain there's shine!'

Charlotte Huggins

The Annual Sheerness Lifeboat Fun Run
Along the sea wall

Sunday 18th September

Linda Rogout

Linda Rogout

Linda Rogout

'Raindrop necklace'
Cobweb on teasles, Barton's Point, Sheerness

Paul Hoggins

Richard Jeferies

Friday 23rd September

Queen's Road looking towards Windmill Rise
Minster

Linda Rogout

'Waiting to surf' Minster Leas   **Saturday 24th September**

Kaj Steffensen

Keeping Sheerness beaches
clean throughout the summer season

Julia McDougall

Julia McDougall

New school development, Isle of Sheppey Academy West Site, Sheerness

Julia McDougall

Julia McDougall

Autumn sun rises to coat us with its golden glory

Julia McDougall

This page has been sponsored by Julia McDougall for the SSAFA Forces

'Sunset Harbour' Queenborough   Friday 30th September

Carolin Galvin

Carolin Galvin

James Apps

The Royal Hotel, Sheerness

James Apps

James Apps

Corinne Michot

This page has been sponsored by Jo Eden. For my late partner Roger.

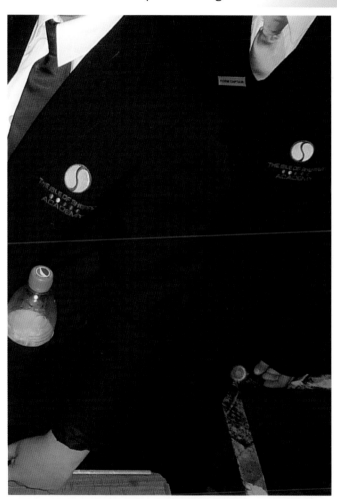

Corinne Michot

The Steel Works

James Apps

This page has been sponsored by The Sittingbourne & Sheppey Conservative Future branch
celebrating the 14th anniversary of the National CF Organisation

The Dockyard Church from the Sea Wall   Saturday 8th October

Linda Rogout

Thistle Hill Way, Minster

Linda Rogout

Julia McDougall

'Sky on fire'

Corinne Michot

Carolin Galvin

'Happy 25th Birthday Tree!'
Junction of Minster Road and Sunnyside Avenue

Linda Rogout

Trevor Jones

Saturday 15th October   'Unveiled by the tide'

Carolin Galvin

Traffic stops for a tug to pass
under The Kings Ferry Bridge

Sunday 16th October

Carolin Galvin

Monday 17th October

Birthday picnic lunch
Bunny Bank at The Glen

Julia McDougall

Nikki Coppins

'I always fancy a man in uniform'
RNLI collection, Tesco's, Sheerness

Julia McDougall

Julia McDougall

'Autumn Morning' Minster sea-front

Marlies Haselton

Julia McDougall

Julia McDougall

Jo Eden

'So there is a green one, a blue one
and a brown one and they're all fifty!'

Julia McDougall

Julia McDougall

Thursday 27th October   'Wild Sunrise'

Jo Eden

Julia McDougall

'Bewitched!'

Julia McDougall

'The best pumpkin'   Sunday 30th October

Linda Brinklow

'In the red' Big Fish Halloween ghost night

James Apps

James Apps

Beach pebble plaque to 365 Project

Julia McDougall

'An interior window into our past' Thursday 3rd November

Julia McDougall

Roy, Two Suns fish merchants, Queenborough

Paul Hoggins

'Sparklers bridge all age groups'   Saturday 5th November

Julia McDougall

Along the bridge from the train

Corinne Michot

Linda Rogout

'Remembering those not here today'

Julia McDougall

'So! On the count of three we take off!'   Wednesday 9th November

Julia McDougall

'Spider's web in the pink sky'

Corinne Michot

Linda Rogout

Nikki Coppins

Julia McDougall

Nikki Coppins

Nikki Coppins

Julia McDougall

Julia McDougall

'On the brink' cliff erosion at Warden Bay

Carolin Galvin

Julia McDougall

'Morning dew'

Caroline Price

Julia McDougall

WW2 building after falling 100ft
from the eroded cliff at Warden Bay

Carolin Galvin

Julia McDougall

Driftwood with oyster shells at Shellness

Julia McDougall

Julia McDougall

Corinne Michot

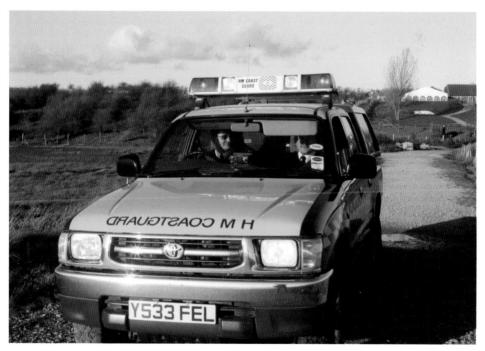

James Apps

Horses in winter clothes

Corinne Michot

James Apps

Corinne Michot

James Apps

'Don't fence me in' Halfway

James Apps

'Winter Larder' Saturday 3rd December

Paul Hoggins

Julia McDougall

Corinne Michot

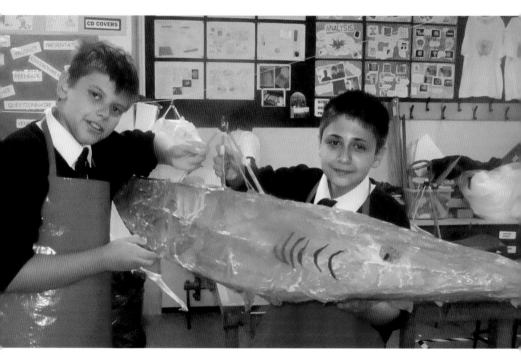

Chris Reed

Julia McDougall

'The Isle of Sheep?' Typical island scene

Julia McDougall

James Apps

Corinne Michot

Corinne Michot

'Iron Sheppey Birds' Industrial area
near the docks from Sheppey bridge

Corinne Michot

Decoration in front garden, Sheerness   Tuesday 13th December

Julia McDougall

Wednesday 14th December   'Caged Santas' Whelans, Blue Town

James Apps

Julia McDougall

Nathalie Banaigs

This page has been sponsored by Gordon Henderson, MP for Sittingbourne & Sheppey with thanks to Kent Creative Arts for including him in their 365 project

Corinne Michot

Julia McDougall

'Dawn Frost' The sun rises over Minster   Monday 19th December

Paul Hoggins

Julia McDougall

Julia McDougall

Carolin Galvin

Julia McDougall

'Unexpected Guest'
Pheasant makes an appearance in the garden

Paul Hoggins

Lights round the Clock Tower in Sheerness   Sunday 25th December

Linda Rogout

Queenborough High Street

Linda Rogout

Linda Rogout

Julia McDougall

Julia McDougall

United in support over demolition'

Julia McDougall

The whole cast of 'Dick Whittington'
The Island Performing Arts Group

Saturday 31st December

Linda Rogout

For another exhibition of style and technical expertise, drop by our showroom.

EuroCanterbury are proud sponsors of the three 'Year in the Life' exhibitions of local photography.

Volkswagen Golf, Fort Mount, Margate.

EuroCanterbury

Broad Oak Road, Canterbury, CT2 7QH.
Telephone: 01227 826800.
www.eurocanterbury.volkswagen.co.uk
**Monday – Saturday 8.30am – 6pm
Sunday 10am – 4pm**
Motability

Kent's Creative Coast

Escape to Create on
Kent's Creative Coast

www.kentcreativecoast.co.uk

View media from a different perspective

From Hougham to Hoo, Chilham to Charing and Biddenden to Birchington, the KM Group know Kent inside out. KM Group's newspapers, websites and radio are produced in Kent by people who really understand the county which means that we are trusted by listeners and readers alike. This means that together KM Group media reaches over **529,304** people each week. That's **38%** of all adults in Kent.*

So if you're looking to reach more customers perhaps it's time to look at things differently. To find out more about our flexible, cost-effective media solutions get in touch with the KM Group Sales team on **01634 227817** or email us at **created@thekmgroup.co.uk** or visit **www.kentonline.co.uk/createdinkent**

Media: Created in Kent

Together we make a **difference**

www.brfm.net   Telephone: 01795 874422   Email: studio@brfm.net

...proud sponsor of
A Year in the Life of Sheppey